My People Redux

poems by

Angela Trudell Vasquez

Finishing Line Press
Georgetown, Kentucky

My People Redux

Copyright © 2022 by Angela Trudell Vasquez
ISBN 978-1-64662-729-5 First Edition
All rights reserved under International and Pan-American Copyright Conventions. No part of this book may be reproduced in any manner whatsoever without written permission from the publisher, except in the case of brief quotations embodied in critical articles and reviews.

ACKNOWLEDGMENTS

I thank the editors of the following journals/organizations for accepting and publishing these poems in print or online:

East on Central: "Goose Eggs" & "What I Found"
FACEBOOK: "Everybody is somebody's child," shared online for International Women's Day by writer
{Insert Title Here}—Literature and Art from the Institute of American Indian Arts: "But I Want Everyone to Know I Am Still Alive," & "Raven"
Subtle Forces—"Once in Seattle
Through This Door—"Everybody is somebody's child"
Yellow Medicine Review: "After the First Snow," "Child Pose Cannot Hold," "Farther Out the Line," "On Loyalty," & "They Could Be Sisters"
Woodland Pattern Book Center (online): "The Congregation," "Maize Maiden," "On Loyalty," & "Raven"

Publisher: Leah Huete de Maines
Editor: Christen Kincaid
Cover Art: Angela Trudell Vasquez
Author Photo: Devin P. Trudell
Cover Design: Elizabeth Maines McCleavy

Order online: www.finishinglinepress.com
also available on amazon.com

Author inquiries and mail orders:
Finishing Line Press
PO Box 1626
Georgetown, Kentucky 40324
USA

Table of Contents

They Could Be Sisters 1

Kick the Can 2

After the First Snow 4

Goose Eggs 5

My People Redux 6

Everybody is somebody's child 10

Maize Maiden 12

Child Pose Cannot Hold 13

What I Found 15

Standing in Line at the Library of Congress 16

But I want everyone to know I am still alive 18

Once in Seattle 19

The Congregation 20

Blizzard 22

The Altar 23

Raven 24

Farther Out the Line 25

Epilogue

On Loyalty 27

"I am looking for a way to vocalize, perform, act out, address the commonly felt crises of my time. These are spiritual exercises."
C.D. Wright, Cooling Time

They Could Be Sisters…

Three girls with straight
waist-length black hair
go round and round the circle.
They cycle, talk, sing—
locks whip in their wake
sunlight highlights
red handlebar streamers.
Spinning on two wheels,
they split, jump curbs, catch air.

To fly or flee or speed
perched high and free
on a purple banana seat.
This is where my power
started flowing   on a bike
in the driver's seat.
The three roll on grass
when a voice echoes. Shouting
distance rules. Close the drapes.

Kick the Can

Trains rattle across Four Mile Creek
carry livestock to feed the hungry machine.

Swimming in flooded cornfields   we crawl through DDT.

Mulberries purple stain ooze through bare toes,
starburst heels. Mosquitos buzz in our ears—

feed on limbs, bite under shorts. Ticks land
on our heads cause night body inspections.

Corn arms scratch our legs as we run through farmers'
young rows play   find the scarecrow, the hobo.

We cut off kids play   kick the can   under earthshine
     cry out in the soft blue dark.

Sweet clover, dandelions, oak trunks
know our names as we dangle—

from stripped limbs   dive off at six feet.
I am nine, the ringleader, the *I know* girl.

We tell ghost stories, hunt for clues, peer into panes
little ones stand on shoulders to see   report back.

We trample earth paths, search for caves,
sunken farm houses, old graves. Sometimes—

semis tip over and hooves clatter up
our dead end street, earth crashing roar

nostril thunder   snorts   steam…
Cows and horses destined for meat packing plants

plot for freedom, pass under our window frames
their last chance hangs.

Mothers run out of their kitchens scoop stunned toddlers
from the middle of the stampede

remark how often this happens   animals
breaking semi steel doors.

Winegardner Road   where underground railroads ran
and good Iowans hid refugees in root cellars

in between fake walls, civil wars
until the next train crossed the land,

the creek, loess fields   straight line from China
spine of tundra. Trains still rattle

carry oil, soybeans.   And children
stub their toes bloody all summer play

kick the can   barefoot on concrete
moisture riding their back, sweat beads

the second they leave the shower. Reporters—
crack eggs on sidewalks   the whites steam…

After the First Snow

Bushes shake white gifts. Fleck flecks.
               Earth quakes.

Pine, oak, maple trees dance lift limbs, bow
burning bush trembles with each footstep   droplets thunder.

Icicles on my birthday sparkle, clear candles.
Icy breath of pine cones, each branch breathes out   clean.

Dust off flakes give thanks to the trunks who let me linger
in their froth, a child again beneath this skin package.

Winter's tongue landscapes the morning, silver palette—
sleds come out of storing children shriek, flock
to the hill carve runs all afternoon, sweaty kid brows shine.

Goose Eggs

Fifteen siblings orphaned.
Eldest, she absorbed:
the kids, kitchen, laundry,
baked bread, made
stone fruit pies,
lemon meringue,
banana cream—
until she died.

Thighs aside saddle
on her tricycle
pedaling to the diner,
she delivered
artful peaks.

Holidays,
she doled
out hot bread
in the corner,
hand sliced,
country buttered.

An Easter of hard boiled
goose eggs. We gnawed
on them for weeks
two handed.

Christmas,
over fifty of us,
in one room.
Everyone, got
five dollars,
a card signed,
Love, Grandma Alice.
Though we,
were not blood…

My People Redux

I.

Crossed rivers and high deserts
before water jugs littered parched lands—
rode motorbikes, carried *comals*, seeds,
black and white photographs.

Fought poor villagers on their homelands
went from high school to the front lines.
Lessons on patriotism led to flag burning,
joints lit, alcoholic stupors, streaking.
        A roll of the dice:
        heads I live, tails I leave.

My people, forgot they rose from the earth.

II.

Our great-grandpa knew
he planted corn rows
praying while he weeded
and walked between
his crooked lines,
singing to the clouds to come
lay their rain music down,
drum a new rhythm
tap the green stalks to grow.
He wove a footpath
from the back door
to the smallest plant
whispering its name
and fed his family
with what he wrought
from earth and aqua sky,
what he coaxed between loam
and hard copper hands.

III.

His kind fingers twist off pears, peppers,
slender green beans, husks of sweet corn,
crab apples and peaches—
what the white tailed deer did not nibble.

Bees buzz in their hive
lured by the burnt man who croons at dawn,
by his wife who brings him *pan dulce*
and black cream in the morning
in her pink house dress and potato sack apron.

Leather patched by sun in scarecrow clothes
muscles cling to his bones. Never young.
Family a heavy wool blanket covers his sins in the heat.

Blessed with grandchildren, they run in his rows,
bring him home books he cannot read. Pages
telling a history he corrects after cartoons each day.

IV.

Great grandchildren search for his buried grave
armed with spades and hoes
so they know where they came from
and can find their way back
to the original place of green grace
mountain breath, stews cooked with seeds
woven into a young girl's black braid
sewn in the hem of her deer dress.

Everybody is somebody's child

For the woman who swims on her back
baby floating on her breasts, eyelashes facing the stars.

For the girl who walks three miles for fresh water,
gourd atop of her head, bare feet on earth.

For the mother who shields her child with board games
and hot chocolate from falling cluster bombs.

Whose fingers read coins and sauté—
red peppers, onions, gifts bought at the open air market.
Who quarters tomatoes from the stand along the road,
roasts sweet corn from the back of a pickup truck
on a lost country highway from a woman folded in half.

The widow who hiked for days
holding on with both hands two smaller than her own,
another one strapped on her back with a bottle,
stopped at a border due to the wrong stamp
and offices closed for the holiday.

The strangers who found her crying on a side road,
a couple who crossed the Rio Grande with her later
when the moon shone, though they had papers.
Toddler perched on the man's shoulders, finger tips dangling
bags for precious lives, snacks, water for the journey.

The grandmother who watches her grandchildren
while their parents work outside the home,
teaches them to share building blocks
how to read, walks them to the park
to see the squirrels and ducks
on the pond scatter at their joyful cries
short legs scrambling down the bank.

The woman who rides the waves
and prays the rickety boat will reach
Lesbos' shores, and on the other side waits:
warm bread, lentil soup, tea with honey,
coffee, a bed to sleep, people
who will throw open their doors
and *let them in, let them in...*

Maize Maiden
(After Rex Lee Jim)

Wait *chica* listen
press knees
lips ears to earth floor

corn
in the beginning
corn in the end

green arms
dance in rows
ancestor whispers
shed pollen in wind

years of plenty
stories fill bowls
children grow long
tomorrow's seeds rest indoors.

Child Pose Cannot Hold

Shaken core
      faith   falls to floor,
hollow where once her heart beat—
pores soak heat body runs cold,
blind, I fill out forms   with holes.

Lost,   still one pant leg at a time
she tries on belief. Sisters
lift her up in yogic steam.
Child pose cannot hold her.

She pays bills, writes checks,
remembers the adored—
      why it is not enough.
Does the daily chores, showers,
feeds and waters.

She dances, pretends
      all is fine—
packs suit cases for no arrivals,
looks for confidence
in her bureau,
like the real twin she once had.

I know what I have lost
deep in glass and star horses
      watch sun rise   fall
let waves wash, ankle crushing rocks—
pain keeps me alive. One cries pretends it is rain.

With good news—
she makes designs to go away
leave sad girl behind
with hair streaked gray,
pulls poems from marrow for travel.

Pine smell, word rivers,
turkey crows, rabbits—
who plow holes,
poetry props spine
when she would cave.

Lies grow long
as silent summer nights.
She knows he does not want her.
Though the words cross his lips.

In it like never before,
neck deep   she pores over sheets,
makes sense of petroglyphs
found in notebooks,
tries to recapture   what she meant to say.

She crawls to the finish line,
back hurts, tears come uncalled
writhes with self-doubt,
wriggles in blankets cannot sleep
tries to recall her name.

Birthday comes goes
in a wave of turkey and booze.
More poses, less dance—

still letters carved out of my forehead
    spill on the page.

End with a few good lines.
Papers, wrote. Deceit, billows
    She thinks—

she is an island   where words marry,
witness creation, lava flows.

What I Found

Sun worshipping lizards lounging on volcanic rocks, stone walls, rebar patches, snatches of fisherman nets, bottle caps, pirates' nests. Iguanas zip on marble floors, hide in cool stucco houses, stroll in manicured gardens with split tongues, stop traffic. A loose way of walking, the island roll of the hips, lips to sing "Black Magic Woman" in Spanish, Latin roots tuning the bars of my crib. Mango juice for breakfast, pork tamales, marigold yolks, cream filled *pan dulces* that spill when you bite. Motorbikes balancing four heartbeats, pocket dogs, grandmas and girls. Turquoise casas that mirror the Caribbean somersault towards the sea. Washing dishes in yellow porcelain sinks under the back stairs, rolling under stars.
Sea breeze dried saucers. Wind whipped towels.
Fishermen who float at dawn. The sky tangerine.
No wooden boat just bodies on water.

Standing in Line at the Library of Congress
    (for my new friend   an arts patron)

Our hands carry no books for the poet laureate   but *mucho* gratitude.

We stand   two free women bridging distances   me, child of Mexicans, she, child of DC.

Cherries blossom. The White House blooms across the street.

She is single. Moved to California, came home to DC. Tells me all the museums are free. How citizens revolted when a dollar was floated clogged the subway with signs, beat back the fees.

Immaculate white marble.

She says, *look at this craftsmanship*. We pause. Give thanks
to the nameless artisans, her ancestors, those who sculpted
this grand building on stolen land where we queue now with wine
and cheese waiting to lay eyes on, mix speech, blessings
with the first Chicano poet laureate of the United States.

We share favorite writers, family stories. How they tried to kick out
mine. How they enslaved hers. The history of this place.
The line winds down   it's past late. We lie to the aide
who inquires *yes, we have books to sign*. We wait to press hands palms
flesh mingle aspirations with the migrant worker boy who grew up
to be poetry king who planted corn rows with his family, whose term
was just extended another two years in this hallowed structure
borne of flesh sweat blood tears and bone   bodies stacked/secrets
in every crevice a president holds court across the street deports
asylum seekers with a decree   mothers, fathers, stretch
arms across barbed wire   weep rivers and streams along the
fence   babies suckle blankets   not their mother's breasts.

This is an old practice   child, parent   filial separations. The body
remembers tears flood our eyes. We look away, come back
memories alive in our DNA spirals   so like the Milky Way.

We get close, shake hands, embrace, get ready to take our leave,
depart. First her, then me.

Our people   hover close with no feet float among us stragglers
carry no more grief.

I leave with this poem   train to the hostel.

But I want everyone to know I am still alive
(After Lorca)

I blow about the trees
inhale dandelion heads
visit when you would rather
pick up a rope than a pen
I come to you when you
droop on stone steps
swim in your water
your food your soil
my body floats in rain clouds
you breathe me
through your nostrils
I am apple's flower scent
arugula's bitter taste
a malty sip of beer
the pungent god giving aroma
of morning coffee dripping
I swing on monkey bars climb trees
sit on your shoulder
stroke hair behind your ears
and when you write late
kiss the air around your face.

Once in Seattle

Car wheels, bikes, delivery
trucks halt mid cycle—
traffic lights cease to blink.
While forward motion splits itself apart
and reassembles, the troll winks
from under the Aurora bridge
gets up from his hiding spot
puts the VW bug down and stomps off
into Lake Union shoulders descending,
ears ship sails on the horizon.

Earth holds its breath on its axis
during the reboot, then exhales—
I stop holding my breath.
Ask my friend, "Did you feel that?"
She nods. We cross when the light
turns green, order red curry.

Pine trees shake off their cones,
magnolia blossoms quiver,
white seagulls' flight patterns
continue. The scavengers dive
bomb lunch revelers' avocado
sandwiches in tech plaza.

The Congregation

Stained glass walls, hard wood floors.

Parking lot chickens watch from behind wire, shuffle back and forth as if we were the zoo animals and not them penned in a cage.

Old church now fitness center, facials, acupuncture, Zumba dancers, psychedelic tea with mushrooms carry worshippers away.

Blond heads swivel at the dark ones as they pass.

People passing peer in see women dancing to music no one can hear leaping, spinning, shaking hips, grinding, worshipping.

In the hall a person ruffles through coat pockets looking for a phone, wings become daggers, eyes glow—no one knows no one takes its pleasure from being naughty, peeking.

People used to worship here and pastor ghosts cavort watch comings and goings. What happened to the steeple, the organ, the people? Now this old church carved back to empty.

Shadows join the dancers, there should be twenty shadows but there is close to fifty all the parishioners have joined in the dance and the dancers do not see their numbers have grown.

Ghosts do not grow short of breath or sweat they go under upraised legs, crawl under knees, sniff the necks of the women so alive, lick raised armpits, remember how it was to be in bone, skin, skeleton, to sweat, to bleed, to spin bare feet on floor and peel off the calluses from the day before. This is living. Old witches now kin.

The music stops the dancers collapse in their skin, revelers hold hands, fragments of old cling to real life.

Hard wood floors shine wet, stained glass walls shake, shimmer, light bathes dancers' chests heaving.

Blizzard

Rolling blind no white lines, no light no
streets, snow beneath my wheels five inches
deep I cannot see ice pelts me, 'Where am I?"
My eyes search for a glimmer of green.
"Please let me be going straight not crossing."

Iowa ice storm legends, tree
limbs crack through roofs.
My car spins into a ditch—
the shame-ride back with a stranger.

Worst stretch, closest to home.
I could be driving off road chasing death.
Howling wind beats the gold car. Alone.
I pray. 'Hail Mary full of grace…"
A child again chanting, chasing
ghosts from my bedroom,

or driving home with my parents
on Christmas night in a storm.
Ice roads, no sand trucks, no salt.
My dad swerves. My mom grabs
the wheel. "We were crossing."
Me, a kid in the back with my sisters.

I cast the rosary over dashboard.
Bridge cover my savior, highway—
splits ahead turn steer plow
metal, rubber against wet
take the next exit tires spin,
slip carry me to bed.

The Altar

Rabbit returns
blue night sky
brick blood clay.

Asleep among the kale, the white tail
falls back to the garden.

      Campus oasis.

Where bare hands mound red dirt
cup earth moisture
fingertips to seed to soil

breath whispers   *grow, grow*

mecca for the bobcat stalker
home of ravens who soar sing
protest in sync
loud tracks zig zag
trace wing prayers
for the living
acres of silt, shadows
in the high desert valley.

Raven

My niece forged in the belly of her mother
island corn child, doughy flesh, white unlike me
seed of Chinese merchant sailor,
Taino natives hiding in interior trees,
of pancake hands and tortilla minds
of plantains shaped in balls fried pork inside,
curls the size of grapefruits eyes of jade
crawling on her knees she shoves her German Shepherd away
as if he was a fly not 150 pounds of flesh fur desire,
she began walking one day tottering between piano legs sofa couches
her fresh skin springs back unlike the hard *churros* sold next door
she laughs at her brother plays with his cast aside awards,
looks less like my sister more like her father's tribe
carries thumbprints of a people
down nostrils, black hair, green eyes,
she will learn how Puerto Rico keeps getting stolen
how Mexico has risen, fallen, about blood in all soil
living in the barrio she shuffles between
high rises skyscrapers, busses and doormen, valets, *palettas*,
the Michigan Mile, mango sellers, condo dwellers,
to live on this land with one heart is to breathe every day divided.

Farther Out the Line

Backpack billows: hair bows,
fire trucks, picture books,
colored words, paper,
pens and pencils.

I crawl in headphones:
block teenagers clash
of beer cans, baby cries
shattering glass, old men
snores and chain brakes
that shudder at intersections.

Train towns surround tracks:
brew pubs, opera houses,
cappuccino, red and white
pizza parlors, dive bars, psychics—
offer escape, spaces for working
stiffs to flash cash buy cheese
curds, pickled eggs.

Roll clatter steel on wheel
by horse farms, cows.
To be still while moving.
I look for coyotes always,
spy hawks hunting instead,
little gray birds chase crows
from their nests. Feathers
circle overhead, ride air
streams. Wiser birders
know their names. I envy
the span of their wings,
earth bound and rooted.

The farther out the line
the darker the children.
Scooters and bikes
race the locomotive.
Grin when they lose.
I smile back.

Some suburbs have all
white farmer's markets,
dogs with orange
and blue tutus,
high school bands
in polyester,
flags that wave
at a distance—
no one salutes.

Epilogue:

On Loyalty

I write poems

    to save myself

           from drowning,

falling into

    the abyss   of busyness,

to heal   the world

    and me,

to learn what   I am thinking,

so the pen can tap into my brain,

reveal what is hiding,

not to court friends or foes,

but to keep   from   disappearing.

Angie Trudell Vasquez is a Mexican-American writer, a Chicana, and holds an MFA in poetry from the Institute of American Indian Arts where she studied Indigenous Poetics with some of the best Native and Indigenous poets and writers in the world. Finishing Line Press published her third collection of poetry, In Light, Always Light, in 2019, and her fourth collection, *My People Redux* in 2022.

A new Macondista, she is currently working on a collection of new and selected poems to submit that will include all of her books, *The Force Your Face Carries, Love in War Time*, and select poems in anthologies, journals, online and in print. Her poems have appeared in the *Yellow Medicine Review, The Slow Down, the Raven Chronicles, The Rumpus, Taos Journal of Poetry,* on the Poetry Foundation's website, and elsewhere.

She is the current poet laureate of Madison, Wisconsin and the first Latina to hold the position. She recently co-edited a poetry anthology entitled, *Through This Door—Wisconsin in Poems,* with former Wisconsin Poet Laureate, Margaret Rozga, and released it through her small press, Art Night Books, in November 2020. With poet Millissa Kingbird, she co-edited the Spring 2019 issue of the journal the *Yellow Medicine Review.*

You can find more about her and her work at angietrudellvasquez.com, artnightbooks.com or follow her on Facebook where she primarily shares things related to art, history and poetry.

www.ingramcontent.com/pod-product-compliance
Lightning Source LLC
LaVergne TN
LVHW041512070426
835507LV00012B/1525